Thank Two (or Four)

Downsized Recipes for Today's Thanksgiving Dinner

CYNTHIA GRAUBART

Copyright © 2020 CYNTHIA GRAUBART

ISBN: 978-0-9749045-1-1

Empire Press

DEDICATION

This recipe collection is dedicated to medical personnel fighting the Covid-19 pandemic.
A portion of the proceeds of this book is being donated to the Frontline Workers Fund in support of their efforts.

CONTENTS

ACKNOWLEDGMENTS

The digital world has opened up publishing and leveled the playing field. Here's to putting the power in the authors' hands.

Cooking is rarely a solitary activity, and I'm glad my husband Cliff has a great appetite for whatever I dish up. My daughter-in-law Maredith Sheridan and my sister Phylecia Bare were trusted copy editors, and any remaining mistakes are completely my own.

The photographs in this book are my first attempt at food photography. I've got lots to learn, but thanks to Christina Peters, I'm on my way.

DOWNSIZED RECIPES FOR TODAY'S THANKSGIVING DINNER

None of us could picture back in March of 2020 what Thanksgiving would look like. The COVID-19 global pandemic has influenced us in so many ways. This cookbook is for all of the families who are gathering differently this year. It's my hope that you'll find joy in whatever celebration you create.

Holiday traditions are what bind us together as families, family-by-choice, and close friends. When there's a break in tradition, it can be unsettling. Food traditions around holidays are particularly unyielding—we know everyone wants the sweet potatoes prepared by Aunt Kathy, so don't even think of changing that up!

But now we find ourselves in new territory. The casserole that serves 16 we always carry to Mom's house may be the only holiday dish we've ever had to worry about. Celebrating a holiday with just 2 or 4 people needs recipes sized just right.

This recipe collection perfect for downsizing your holiday. It contains the makings of a celebratory meal serving 2 to 4 people. All the courses are right here from comforting casseroles and side dishes, to elegant turkey breasts, homey skillet turkey thighs, and mini pies for dessert. Some of the turkey recipes will yield those beloved leftovers for a second meal or sandwiches. Even if you've never made Thanksgiving dinner before, I know you'll be successful with these easy recipes made with whole foods we love.

No matter how you choose to celebrate, I wish you a happy Thanksgiving.

Cynthia Graubart

THE KEYS TO A DELICIOUS HOLIDAY

Make a Plan
Any celebration goes more smoothly with a plan. Select your
recipes and make a note of baking times and temperatures and plan
your day accordingly. All of the side dishes can be made ahead and
reheated for serving.

Serves Two (or Four)
In parentheses throughout the ingredient lists and directions are
quantities and times if serving 4 people. Most are a straight
doubling of the recipe, but in some cases, only a little extra is
needed. All of those calculations have been done for you.

Thawing
Rejoice! Thawing a turkey breast takes less time than a whole
turkey! But, you'll still need to plan that time.

The Secret Weapon
It's Turkey Stock! No time like the present to make a batch and
package it for the freezer. It defrosts easily in the microwave or on
the stove. Use it in nearly all of the recipes here. Homemade stock
adds a depth of flavor to recipes not easily achieved with canned
stock. It's also handy for keeping leftovers from drying out.

Cooking to Temperature
An instant read thermometer is a cook's best friend. You'll never
worry about whether or not the turkey is done if you are cooking it
to temperature. Rest any cooked turkey a few minutes before
carving.

Overcooking
The best way to avoid over cooking Thanksgiving dishes, in
addition to cooking to temperature, is to cover things that are
browning too quickly with foil. The foil will help preserve moisture
and keep foods from burning.

To Toast, or Not to Toast
All of these recipes are perfectly sized for cooking in a countertop toaster oven. The temperatures are the same. Keep in mind a convection setting will cook food faster, but potentially dry out the surface of the food. Keep foil on hand to cover any fast-browning dishes.

Ingredients
Purchase the best ingredients your food budget allows. Use real butter and cream. Thanksgiving is no time to skimp on calories. Most of these recipes use butter to coat baking dishes, but use oil or a spray if you prefer. The three sisters of Thanksgiving herbs are rosemary, sage, and thyme. They are used liberally throughout the recipes. Substitute the herb combinations freely. Sage is a quintessential Thanksgiving taste. Parsley is terribly underrated and if you are shy about herbs in your cooking, use parsley. It will brighten the flavor of any dish. Mushrooms called for in these recipes may be any you prefer. I often use regular white button mushrooms mixed with shiitakes as my go-to combination.

BONE-IN HERBED TURKEY BREAST

Preparation Time: 15 minutes
Start to Finish Time: 2½ - 3 hours
Serves: 2 - 6

Bone-in turkey breasts provide a festive presentation on a platter in the absence of a full turkey. This turkey breast will easily feed 6 people. If your meal is for a smaller gathering and you enjoy turkey leftovers, carve the meat as desired and freeze in recipe-ready portions for sandwiches and casseroles. After the breast is fully carved, reserve all the bones to make a stock to use in a future soup.

   1 large onion, cut into wedges
   2 celery stalks, roughly chopped
   1 (approx. 6 pound) bone-in turkey breast
   1 tablespoon chopped fresh rosemary

1 tablespoon chopped fresh sage
1 tablespoon chopped fresh thyme
2 tablespoons butter, room temperature
1½ cups turkey or chicken stock or broth
2 tablespoons cornstarch
2 tablespoons water

Heat oven to 425°F. Coat a roasting pan with cooking spray.

Line the bottom of the roasting pan with onion and celery. Dry turkey breast and place on top of vegetables. Stir herbs and butter together and spread over the turkey skin. Season with salt and pepper.

Pour stock in bottom of roasting pan and move pan to oven. Roast breast roughly 20 minutes per pound. Begin testing for doneness after 90 minutes. Baste as desired with pan drippings for a richer colored skin. The breast is cooked when the internal temperature reaches 165°F on an instant read thermometer.

Remove breast from oven and move to a carving board. Let rest 15 minutes before carving.

Pour contents of roasting pan through a strainer over a skillet. Discard solids. Set heat to medium high and bring to a boil. Whisk together cornstarch and water in a small bowl to form a slurry and whisk into the liquid in the skillet. Reduce heat to low. Gravy is ready when thickened. Taste and adjust seasonings as desired. Serve gravy with turkey.

BONELESS TURKEY BREAST WITH
BOURBON-ORANGE GLAZE

Preparation Time: 10 minutes
Start to Finish Time: 1 hour, 45 minutes
Serves: 2 with leftovers, or 4 for main course

A boneless breast is a fuss-free entree for Thanksgiving. It's just right for the main course and suited for those wanting beloved turkey leftovers for another meal or sandwiches. Boneless turkey breasts produce very few drippings, so plan on making gravy while the breast is roasting.

1 (approx. 2 pound) boneless turkey breast
1 tablespoon butter
Salt
Freshly ground black pepper

For the sauce:
1 tablespoon butter
1 garlic clove, minced
1 tablespoon all-purpose flour
1 medium orange, zested and juiced
2 tablespoons brown sugar
¼ cup bourbon
½ cup turkey or chicken stock or broth

Heat oven to 350°F. Fit a small roasting pan with a rack.

Dry turkey breast and move to rack. Coat breast evenly all over with butter. Season roast all over with salt and pepper. Boneless breasts come dressed in a string bag. Leave it in place until after cooking.

Roast breast 90 minutes. Test internal temperature and keep roasting until the interior temperature reaches 165°F on an instant read thermometer. Allow breast to rest 10 minutes before carving. Gently snip the string bag open to carefully remove it, leaving as much skin in place as possible. Slice as desired.

While the breast is roasting, melt butter in a small saucepan over medium heat. Sauté garlic in the hot butter 30 seconds. Whisk in flour and cook until starting to turn light brown and all the white flour is incorporated. Zest and juice a medium orange and pour the juice slowly into the flour, stirring constantly. Whisk in brown sugar, bourbon, and stock, and stir until thickened. Stir zest into remaining gravy and keep warm. If gravy is too thick, adjust with additional stock.

If drippings have collected, add to any gravy made for serving.

SHEET PAN CORNISH HEN THANKSGIVING DINNER

Preparation Time: 15 minutes
Start to Finish Time: 1 hour, 15 minutes
Serves: 2 (or 4)

For a simple, one-pan solution to Thanksgiving, a sheet pan dinner serves up the main dish Cornish hens, and sides of roast potatoes and green beans all in one. Cleaning up after a holiday meal has never been easier! Cornish hens can feed two people, but know your diners as some will eat one whole hen. Splitting the hens is easier with a pair of poultry shears, or other heavy scissors. Two sheet pans will be needed if doubling the recipe.

- ½ (1) pound small potatoes, halved or quartered
- 2 (4) medium onions, each cut into 6 wedges, divided
- 1 (2) lemon, thinly sliced
- 2 (4) tablespoons olive oil, divided

2 (4) Cornish hens
3 tablespoons butter, divided
4 (8) fresh rosemary sprigs
4 (8) fresh thyme sprigs
Salt
Freshly ground black pepper
½ pound fresh green beans, trimmed
1 (2) leek, trimmed, white part thinly sliced, rinsed well
2 sprigs parsley
2 tablespoons all-purpose flour

Heat oven to 425°F. Spray a rimmed baking sheet with cooking spray. If doubling the recipe, prepare two baking sheets.

Toss the potatoes and nine of the onion wedges with the oil in a medium bowl. Spread out on baking sheet. Top with lemon slices.

Pat hens dry and cut up either side of backbones to remove. Save for stock (see below, or freeze if using later), or discard. Rub outside of hens with 1 tablespoon of the butter and place skin side up over potatoes and lemons. Slip a rosemary sprig under each hen.

Move baking sheet to hot oven and roast 30 minutes. Toss green beans and leeks in remaining tablespoon oil and scatter over potatoes around hens. Roast an additional 20 minutes, until the thickest part of the thigh on a hen reaches 170°F on an instant read thermometer.

While the hens are roasting, make a quick stock for gravy. Brown the backbones skin-side down in a saucepan over medium heat. When browned, add 3 cups water, remaining onion wedges, and parsley sprigs. Increase the temperature to high and bring to a boil. Reduce heat to low and simmer until hens are cooked.

When hens have come to temperature, remove from oven and either serve from the sheet pan, or transfer hens to a serving platter and move vegetables to a serving dish.

Melt the remaining 2 tablespoons butter in a skillet over medium-high heat. Whisk in flour and keep whisking to fully incorporate and mixture has turned nearly dark brown. The color of this mixture, the roux, will help color the gravy. Slowly stir in the stock, whisking vigorously until smooth and the gravy has thickened. Serve with hens and vegetables.

Variation:
Substitute peeled and diced sweet potatoes for the small potatoes.

(BLANK)

SKILLET TURKEY THIGHS IN SAGE MUSHROOM GRAVY

Preparation Time: 15 minutes
Start to Finish Time: 2 hours
Serves: 2 (or 4)

This satisfying dish works any time of year, but is lovely during the holidays with its luscious, meaty gravy. Thighs can be quite large, so one large thigh may serve two people.

    1 (2) tablespoon olive oil
    2 (4) tablespoons butter, divided
    2 (4) turkey thighs
    Salt
    Freshly ground black pepper
    ½ (1) small onion, chopped
    1 (2) small stalk celery, chopped
    8 (16) ounces mushrooms, halved and quartered

½ (1) cup white wine

4 - 6 (8 - 12) fresh sage leaves, chopped,
    plus more for garnish

1 - 2 (2 - 3) cups chicken or turkey stock or broth

2 (3) tablespoons cornstarch

2 (3) tablespoons water

Heat a large skillet with a lid over medium high heat. When hot, add the oil and butter. Season the turkey thighs on both sides with salt and pepper. Brown the thighs in the hot fat skin side down first, until golden. Turn and brown second side about 3 minutes. Remove thighs to a plate.

Add onion and celery to the same skillet and cook 5 to 7 minutes, stirring frequently. Stir in the mushrooms and cook about 4 minutes to lightly cook the mushrooms. Stir in the wine and sage and scrape up any bits in the pan. Return the thighs to the pan, skin side up.

Pour enough stock into the pan to come halfway up the side of the thighs. Reduce heat to a simmer. Cover and cook about 90 minutes, until the thickest part of the thigh reaches 175°F on an instant read thermometer. Remove the thighs to a clean platter.

Whisk together the cornstarch and water in a small bowl to form a slurry. Stir this slurry into the remaining sauce. Increase the heat to medium high. Stir the sauce until it boils. Remove from heat and return thighs to the skillet or pour the sauce into a serving vessel and serve alongside the thighs. Garnish with extra sage leaves if desired.

DIJON TURKEY TENDERLOIN

Preparation Time: 5 minutes
Start to Finish Time: 45 minutes
Serves: 2 (or 4)

Turkey tenderloins are the quickest-cooking part of the turkey. Located under the breast, the tenderloin is an all white meat part of the turkey and won't dry out as it bakes in this bath of white wine and Dijon mustard.

 1 (2) turkey tenderloin
 1 (2) tablespoon butter, room temperature
 Salt
 Freshly ground black pepper
 ½ (1) cup white wine
 1 tablespoon Dijon mustard
 4 (8) ounces mushrooms, sliced
 1 ½ (2) teaspoon fresh oregano leaves

1 (2) tablespoon cornstarch
1 (2) tablespoon water

Heat oven to 375°F. Coat a small baking dish with cooking spray.

Pat the tenderloin dry and rub with butter. Season as desired with salt and pepper.

Heat a skillet over medium high heat. When hot, add tenderloin and brown the first side about 4 to 5 minutes. Turn and brown second side about 3 - 4 minutes. Move the tenderloin to the prepared baking dish.

Whisk together the mustard and wine in a small bowl. Pour into the bottom of the dish. Scatter mushrooms around tenderloin. Sprinkle the tenderloin and mushrooms with the oregano.

Bake 35 - 40 minutes, until the thickest part of the tenderloin registers 170°F on an instant read thermometer. Let tenderloin rest 5 minutes before slicing.

If desired, move the pan sauce to a saucepan over medium-high heat. Whisk together the cornstarch and water in a small bowl to form a slurry. Stir the slurry into the sauce and stir until it comes to a boil and thickens. Remove from heat, taste and adjust seasoning as desired, and serve with the sliced tenderloin.

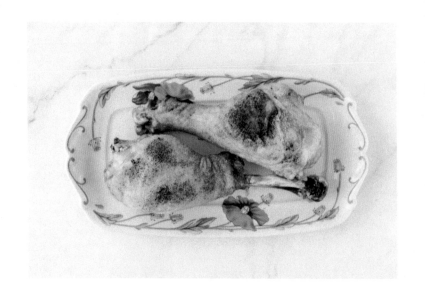

ROAST TURKEY LEGS

Preparation Time: 5 minutes
Start to Finish Time: 1 hour
Serves: 2 (or 4)

Turkey legs are perfect for a small Thanksgiving and also can be useful if dark meat is a desired addition to a turkey breast menu. My mother-in-law Frances loved to coat any poultry skin with garlic powder and this simple recipe is perfect for crispy skin lovers.

2 (4) turkey legs
1 (2) tablespoon butter, room temperature
1 (2) teaspoon garlic powder
Salt
Freshly ground black pepper

Heat oven to 350°F. Line a rimmed baking sheet with parchment paper and set aside.

Pat turkey legs dry and coat with butter. Sprinkle evenly with garlic powder and season with salt and pepper. Move to the prepared baking sheet. Cover tightly with foil and bake 30 minutes.

Remove foil and bake additional 25 - 30 minutes, until the thickest part of the leg registers 170°F on instant read thermometer. Serve hot.

CORNBREAD MUSHROOM DRESSING
WITH SAGE

Preparation Time: 10 minutes
Start to Finish Time:
Serves: 2 (or 4)

No other side dish is more controversial than dressing, or as some say, stuffing. Years ago, I stopped stuffing the turkey and instead just made a pan of dressing. I like being sure that it's fully cooked and not worrying about if any under-done turkey juices are left lingering in my stuffing. Having said that, though, this dressing works equally as well as a stuffing, especially for Cornish hens where the stuffing is fully cooked in the time it takes to properly roast the hens. Some may prefer to substitute a combination of biscuits or white bread in with the cornbread. Suit your taste buds.

4 (8) tablespoons butter, divided
4 (8) ounces mushrooms, roughly chopped
¼ (½) cup chopped onion
1 (2) small celery rib, chopped
1 (2) garlic clove, minced
2 (4) teaspoons chopped fresh sage
2 (4) chopped fresh thyme
2 (4) tablespoons chopped pecans
Salt
Freshly ground black pepper
½ (whole) recipe Cornbread (recipe follows)
2 tablespoons white wine
1 (2) cups turkey or chicken stock or broth

Heat the oven to 350°F. Rub a small baking dish with part of the butter and set aside.

Heat a skillet over medium heat. When hot, add 1 tablespoon of the butter and sauté mushrooms until lightly browned. Remove to a large bowl.

Add another 1 tablespoon butter to the skillet and when melted, sauce onion and celery until softened and onion is translucent, about 5 minutes. Stir in garlic, sage, thyme, and pecans. Season with salt and pepper and cook 2 minutes. Add to bowl with mushrooms. Melt another 1 tablespoon of butter in the hot skillet and set aside.

Toss cornbread with the mushroom-vegetable mixture. Pour melted butter over mixture, toss, and spoon mixture into prepared baking dish. Pour about ½ cup of the stock over the mixture. If it seems dry, add another ¼ cup.

Cover baking dish with foil and move to the oven and bake 40 minutes, until heated through. If a crunchy top is desired, uncover casserole the last 10 minutes of baking time. If casserole seems dry, add another ¼ cup stock and bake until hot. Serve warm. Extra broth or gravy may be needed when reheating leftovers.

Variation:
Crumble and sauté two breakfast link sausages and add to mushroom-vegetable mixture before adding cornbread.

CORNBREAD

Preparation Time: 5 minutes
Start to Finish Time: 30 minutes
Makes: 1 (6 - 7-inch round cornbread)

Cornbread dressing is a traditional side dish all across the south. For best results, bake the cornbread a day or two ahead, cut into cubes, and allow to air dry. If making the Cornbread Dressing for two, only half of the cornbread will be used. Serve the other half at another meal or freeze for later use.

2 tablespoons butter
1 cup yellow cornmeal
½ teaspoon baking powder
½ teaspoon baking soda
½ teaspoon salt
½ cup milk, or buttermilk
1 large egg

Heat oven to 400°F. Add butter to a 6 - 7-inch cast iron skillet and move to oven to heat.

Whisk together the cornmeal, baking powder, baking soda, and salt in a medium mixing bowl. In a separate bowl, whisk the milk, egg, and butter together until smooth. Pour the egg mixture into the cornmeal mixture and stir until just combined.

Remove hot skillet carefully from oven and pour butter into batter and stir. Pour batter into hot buttered skillet. Return to oven and bake 20 to 25 minutes, until the top begins to brown and a cake tester inserted in the center comes out with only a crumb or two. Remove from oven to cool. Turn the cornbread out of the skillet and cut into 1-inch chunks. Spread out on a baking sheet to dry out for about a day.

BUTTERMILK
BRUSSELS SPROUTS CASSEROLE

Preparation Time: 20 minutes
Start to Finish Time: 1 hour
Serves: 2 (or 4)

*This recipe was developed by my friend and colleague
Angie Mosier. It has been on my holiday table for years. I
hope it will make it in your regular holiday menu, too.*

   ¾ (1 ½) pound small Brussels sprouts, trimmed and
      halved
   3 (6) tablespoons unsalted butter, softened, divided
   1 (2) teaspoon finely grated lemon zest
   1 (1) teaspoon lemon juice
   1 (2) tablespoon diced onion
   1 (1) garlic clove, minced
   Salt and freshly ground black pepper

1 (2) tablespoon all-purpose flour
¼ (½) cup buttermilk
1 (2) teaspoon dry mustard (or regular mustard)
½ (1) teaspoon freshly grated nutmeg
⅓ (½) cup grated Parmesan cheese, divided
⅓ (½) cup crumbled Ritz or saltine cracker
1 (2) tablespoon chopped flat-leaf parsley

Heat oven to 350°F.

Steam Brussels sprouts in a steamer basket over boiling water until they are bright green, about 2 to 3 minutes. Rub the inside of a small (medium) baking dish with about 1 teaspoon butter. Move the Brussels sprouts to the baking dish and toss with lemon zest and juice, onion, and garlic. Season with salt and pepper.

Melt 1 (2) tablespoon of the butter in a small saucepan and stir in flour. Whisk and continue cooking until the flour barely starts to brown. Add the buttermilk, whisking to break up any lumps. Add the dry mustard, nutmeg, and ¼ teaspoon of salt and a few grinds of black pepper. Whisk until slightly thick. Add the onion mixture and ½ of the Parmesan to the sauce and stir until they're all incorporated. Pour the mixture over the Brussels sprouts and stir to coat.

Melt the remaining butter in the microwave. Combine the crushed crackers with the remaining Parmesan cheese, parsley, and melted butter. Sprinkle evenly over the top of the casserole. Move to the center rack of the heated oven and cook until bubbly and golden brown, about 25 minutes.

SKILLET GREEN BEANS WITH PECAN BROWNED BUTTER

Preparation Time: 5 minutes
Start to Finish Time: 15 minutes
Serves: 2 (or 4)

I've been on a mission to convert cooks to charring green beans in a skillet. Faster than roasting, the beans stay slightly crispy and maintain their color. The burnished spots contribute a complexity to the overall flavor of the beans. Splitting the fat between butter and olive oil ensures the butter won't burn while the beans are charring.

- 2 (4) tablespoons butter, divided
- 1 (2) tablespoon olive oil
- ½ (1) pound green beans, tipped, tailed, and stringed (if needed)

2 (4) tablespoons chopped pecans
Salt
Freshly ground black pepper
2 (4) teaspoons fresh thyme leaves

Melt 1 (2) tablespoon of the butter and the olive oil in a
medium skillet. When very hot, add the beans, and cook
until dappled with dark brown. Reduce the heat to low, and
continue cooking a few minutes more, stirring, until the
beans are nearly soft. Remove beans to a platter.

Melt remaining butter in skillet and when foamy, add pecans
and cook, stirring frequently, until fragrant and beginning to
brown, just a minute or two, being careful not to burn the
pecans. Return beans to skillet, toss, and season to taste with
salt and pepper. Season with fresh thyme.

NEW-FASHIONED
GREEN BEAN CASSEROLE

Preparation Time: 10 minutes
Start to Finish Time: 45 minutes
Serves: 2 (or 4)

Any top-ten comfort food list includes the taste of my childhood - green bean casserole. Graduating from can-of-soup casseroles, this dish trades the soup for a sauce created with a sour cream base. (Don't worry. I kept the French-fried onions.) Prepare this dish the day of serving, or one day ahead, as the sour cream separates if frozen.

   ½ (1) pound green beans, trimmed
   1 (2) tablespoon butter
   ½ (1) small onion, chopped
   2 - 3 (4 - 6) ounces mushrooms, sliced
   1 (2) garlic clove, minced

1 (2) tablespoon all-purpose flour
Salt
Freshly ground black pepper
½ cup turkey or chicken stock or broth
½ (1) cup sour cream
2 (4) tablespoons milk
2 (4) tablespoons grated cheddar cheese
1 cup French-fried onions, divided

Heat oven to 350°F. Spray a small casserole dish with cooking spray.

Salt a pot of water and put over high heat and bring to a boil. Add green beans and cook just 3 minutes. Drain and run under cold water.

Heat a medium skillet over medium heat. Melt 1 tablespoon butter and stir in raw onion and mushrooms. Cook until onion is translucent, about 5 minutes. Stir in garlic. Sprinkle with flour and stir until flour is completely incorporated with no white specks remaining. Season with salt and pepper.

Pour stock slowly over mushrooms and stir well. Whisk sour cream and milk together and stir into mushroom mixture. Stir in ¼ cup French-fried onions. Stir in green beans.

Transfer bean mixture to prepared baking dish. Top casserole with remaining fried onions and bake until bubbly, about 30 minutes.

SWEET POTATO AND GREENS CASSEROLE

Preparation Time: 10 minutes
Start to Finish Time: 1 hour
Serves: 2 (or 4)

This protein-rich side dish easily serves as a vegetarian main course when doubled. Colorful and full of fall flavor, it's a decadent, hardy dish.

2 (4) medium sweet potatoes
1 (2) tablespoon olive oil
Salt
Freshly ground black pepper
2 (4) tablespoons dry sherry or vermouth
1 (2) garlic clove, minced
1 (2) tablespoon cornstarch
1 (2) cup half-and-half or heavy cream

1 (14-ounce) (or 2) can cannellini beans, rinsed and
        drained
1 (2) large handful chopped fresh kale, about 1 (2) cup
⅓ (⅔) cup grated Parmesan cheese,
        plus 1 (2) tablespoon

Heat oven to 450 green F. Line a rimmed baking sheet with
parchment paper. Spray a small baking dish with cooking
spray.

Peel and slice sweet potatoes in ¼-inch thick slices and toss
with olive oil. Move to prepared baking sheet, season with
salt and pepper, and roast in oven until tender, about 15-18
minutes. Remove from oven and cut into quarters. Reduce
heat to 375°F.

Heat a skillet over medium heat. Add kale and 1 tablespoon
water. Toss until kale is wilted and has begun to soften. Add
sweet potatoes to skillet and toss. Mash half of the cannellini
beans until crushed and add the crushed beans and whole
beans to the skillet. Reduce heat to low.

Heat a small saucepan over medium heat. Add sherry and
garlic and heat until bubbling. Stir cornstarch into cream
and stir into sherry. Stir in Parmesan and stir until mixture
thickens. Remove from heat and stir into greens mixture.

Move mixture to the prepared baking dish and sprinkle with
remaining tablespoon Parmesan cheese. Bake 30 minutes,
until bubbly. Serve warm.

MEMORABLE MASHED POTATOES

Preparation Time: 10 minutes
Start to Finish Time: 25 minutes
Serves: 2 (or 4)

My dear friend and colleague Nathalie Dupree says Thanksgiving is no time to make "skinny" potatoes. Bring on the butter and the cream for memorable mashed potatoes. My grandmother would insist on using white pepper, lest someone think something unpleasant had accidentally slipped into her serving bowl. I stick with black pepper.

1 (2) medium-large Russet potato
    (or 1 (2) pound Yukon gold or other favorite potato)
Salt
3 tablespoons (½ cup) heavy cream

2 tablespoons (¼ cup) butter,
    plus more for serving if desired
Freshly ground black pepper
Freshly chopped chives or parsley, if desired

Peel and chop the potatoes into ½-inch pieces. Add to a medium saucepan and cover with cold water. Salt generously. Bring to the boil over high heat, reduce the heat to low, and simmer 10 to 12 minutes, until the potatoes are fork tender. Before the potatoes finish cooking, warm the cream in the microwave or over low heat in a small saucepan.

When the potatoes are tender, reserve one ladleful of potato water, then drain the potatoes and return to the hot pan over low heat. Add the warm cream and 1 tablespoon of the butter and mash the potatoes using a potato masher, potato ricer, a large fork, or an electric hand mixer. Use reserved potato water to thin potatoes if necessary to achieve desired consistency. Taste and adjust seasonings. Serve warm with extra butter, and top with chopped chives. Leftover potatoes may be reheated in the microwave, or on the stove with a little added water.

SWEET POTATO SOUFFLÉS

Preparation Time: 10 minutes
Start to Finish Time: 45 minutes,
        plus time for baking potatoes
Makes: 2 (1-cup) soufflés (or 4 1-cup)

*Baked in individual ramekins, these single serve soufflés are
a sweet side dish addition to the Thanksgiving table. Sweet
potatoes are sweet on their own, so omit the brown sugar if
you like yours a little less sweet. Marshmallows are
optional, but I do love when they become slightly burnished
on top.*

   2 (4) medium sweet potato, baked or microwaved
        until soft, cooled
   1 (2) teaspoon brown sugar

½ (1) teaspoon ground cinnamon
¼ (½) teaspoon ground ginger
Pinch ground nutmeg
1 (2) large egg, lightly beaten
¼ (½) cup chopped pecans, divided
½ (1) cup mini marshmallows, optional

Heat oven to 350°F.

Mash sweet potato in a medium bowl until smooth. Whisk together the brown sugar, cinnamon, ginger, and nutmeg in a small bowl until thoroughly combined. Stir into sweet potatoes. Using the same small bowl, lightly beat the egg. Stir the egg and half of the pecans into sweet potato mixture.

Divide the mixture between two (four) 1-cup ramekins. Top each with remaining pecans. Move ramekins to baking sheet and bake 30 minutes. If topping with marshmallows, do so 10 minutes before the end of baking time. Serve warm.

Note:
No ramekins? A single small baking dish of any kind will suit.

PULL-APART DINNER ROLLS

Preparation Time: 5 minutes
Start to Finish Time: about 3 hours,
     including rising time
Makes: 4 rolls

*Such little work for such a lovely reward! These dinner
rolls are just right for a holiday table. Put them to use
sopping up gravy and pushing side dishes onto your fork.
This is happiness delivered in a fluffy ball of dough. Coat
the measuring spoon with cooking spray before measuring
the honey and it will slip right out.*

   ¼ cup milk
   2 teaspoons honey
   ½ teaspoon active dry yeast
   2 large egg yolks, divided

1 tablespoon melted butter
1 cup all-purpose flour
¼ teaspoon salt

Heat milk and honey in a small saucepan over low heat until it reaches 115°F (or heat in the microwave). Whisk in the yeast and set aside about 5 minutes, until foamy. Stir in one egg yolk and the melted butter.

Whisk together the flour and salt in a medium bowl. Pour the milk mixture over the flour and stir until combined. Using hands, form the dough into a smooth ball. Cover and let rise, away from drafts, until doubled in size (about 60-90 minutes).

When the dough has risen, spray a 6-inch cake pan or 4 cups of a muffin tin with cooking spray.

Divide the dough into 4 equal pieces and roll each into a smooth, round ball. Move the balls to the cake pan and let dough rise until the rolls are touching, about 1 hour. Heat the oven to 375°F. When the rolls have expanded, brush them with the remaining egg yolk.

Bake on the middle rack of the oven 18-19 minutes, until golden brown. Remove from oven and cool about 5 minutes before serving.

TART CRANBERRY-ORANGE SAUCE

Preparation Time: 10 minutes
Start to Finish Time: 40 minutes
Makes: about 1 (2) cup

The tangy tartness of cranberries is moderated with the addition of maple syrup and an orange liqueur. If liqueur is unavailable, add a little additional syrup.

1 (2) cup fresh cranberries
Zest of 1 (2) small orange
Juice of 1 (2) small orange
½ cup water
1 (2) tablespoon maple syrup,
    or 2 (4) tablespoons granulated sugar
Pinch salt
1 tablespoon orange liqueur, such as Cointreau

Add the cranberries, orange juice, water, maple syrup, and salt to a small saucepan. Bring to a boil over medium-high heat, then reduce the heat to low and simmer about 10 minutes, until the mixture has started to thicken and berries are beginning to burst.

Stir in the orange zest and liqueur and simmer another 10 minutes, stirring occasionally, until the mixture is very thick. Taste and adjust seasonings, if desired. Remove from heat, allow to cool, then store in the refrigerator. Serve cold or room temperature. Cranberry sauce keeps about a week in the refrigerator.

APPLE CRUMBLE

AND

PECAN PIES FOR TWO

Preparation Time: 15 minutes
Start to Finish Time: 1 hour
Makes: one or two 5-inch pies

These pies are perfect for two people. Make one, or make both! For the apple pie, I choose Granny Smith for a tart pie, and for balance I choose Honey Crisp. For the pecan pie, I use dark corn syrup because that's how I grew up. Use light corn syrup if preferred. Depending on the depth of your pie pan, you may have a little filling leftover which can be discarded.

There will be leftover scraps after cutting the pie crusts. They can be cut into decorative shapes, if desired, and sprinkled with cinnamon and sugar for a treat. Bake on a baking sheet about 15 minutes.

1 refrigerated pie crust
1 large egg

For the apple pie:
2 tablespoons granulated sugar
¼ teaspoon ground cinnamon
¼ teaspoon ground ginger
2 - 3 apples, peeled, cored, sliced, and roughly chopped

For the apple pie crumble:
2 tablespoons all-purpose flour
1 tablespoon brown sugar
1 tablespoon granulated sugar
1 tablespoon butter, cut into ¼-inch cubes

For the pecan pie:
¼ cup dark corn syrup
1 large egg
¼ cup granulated sugar
Pinch salt
1 tablespoon butter, melted
½ teaspoon vanilla extract
⅓ cup chopped pecans,
    plus 8 - 10 halves for decorating

Heat oven to 400°F.

Unroll the piecrust on a lightly floured work surface. Roll to
12-inch circle with rolling pin. With 6-inch round cutter, cut
2 rounds from crust. Move one round each to 5-inch pie
pans. Trim any excess crust away with a sharp knife and
decorate edges as desired. Pressing with the tines of a fork is
an easy decoration. Prick bottoms and sides of the pie crust
generously. Separate the egg and discard the yolk. Whisk the
white lightly to break up and brush the inside of the pie
crusts with the egg white. Refrigerate crusts.

For the apple pie:
Whisk together the sugar, cinnamon, and ginger in a
medium bowl. Add sliced apples and toss to coat.

Remove pie crust from refrigerator. Fill pie crust in the pan with apple mixture. Stir together flour, brown sugar, and granulated sugar, and toss with butter cubes. Sprinkle over apples in a pie shell.

Bake pie in the oven on a baking sheet 30 to 40 minutes, until crust is golden brown and filling begins to bubble. Cool pie on cooling rack at least 30 minutes.

For the pecan pie:
Whisk together the corn syrup, egg, granulated sugar, salt, melted butter, and vanilla in a small bowl. Stir in chopped pecans.

Remove pie crust from the refrigerator. Fill pie crust with pecan filling and decorate top with pecan halves.

Bake pie in the oven on a baking sheet 30 minutes, until filling is puffed and pecans are lightly browned. Cool pie on a cooling rack 30 minutes before cutting.

(BLANK)

APPLE PASTRY TARTS

Preparation Time: 10 minutes
Start to Finish Time: 35 minutes
Serves: 6

Every cook needs a quick go-to dessert and these tarts are not only quick - they are beautiful, too. This recipe makes 6 tarts, more than is needed for a Thanksgiving dinner for two. But we must think of breakfast, too, mustn't we?

1 sheet frozen puff pastry, thawed
6 medium apples
¼ cup granulated sugar
2 tablespoon butter, cubed

Heat oven to 425°F. Line a rimmed baking sheet with parchment paper.

Lightly flour a surface and unfold pastry. Cut into 6 (4-inch) squares and move to prepared baking sheet. Prick surface of squares with a fork. Refrigerate while preparing the apples

Core and slice apples thinly and toss with lemon juice in a large bowl. Whisk together the cinnamon and sugar in a small bowl. Sprinkle apples with sugar and toss to coat.

Decorate each square with apple slices, in a decorative pattern if desired. Melt butter and brush over tarts. Bake 20 - 25 minutes, until tarts are puffed, light brown, and apples are tender. Serve warm or room temperature.

Variation: To guild the lily, mix 3 ounces of room temperature cream cheese with 1 tablespoon granulated sugar and 1 tablespoon of water and spread on the pastry before adding the apple slices.

TURKEY STOCK

Preparation Time: 15 minutes
Start to Finish Time: 4 hours
Serves: 2 (or 4)

The foundation of any great Thanksgiving meal is turkey stock. Rich and flavorful, turkey stock turns a plain dish into something special. The basis for great gravy, it's also handy for maintaining moisture in leftovers. Cut the onion with the skin on—it adds color to the stock. Roasting the wings isn't essential, but it, too, adds color to the stock.

  2 (4) turkey wings
  1 (2) tablespoon olive oil
  1 (2) large onion, quartered
  2 (4) carrots, cut into 4 pieces
  2 (4) celery stalks, cut into 4 pieces

4 (8) parsley sprigs
8 (16) whole black peppercorns

Heat oven to 450°F. Coat a rimmed baking sheet with cooking spray.

Toss wings with oil in a large bowl to coat. Move to prepared baking sheet and roast wings until browned, about 25 minutes.

While wings are roasting, pour 6 (12) quarts water into large stock pot. Add onion, carrots, celery, parsley, and peppercorns. Bring to a boil over high heat. When wings are roasted, add to stock pot and reduce heat to low. Simmer stock 3 hours.

Strain stock and discard solids. For richer stock, return strained stock to pot and simmer until stock is reduced by a third. Cool stock and refrigerate. If made more than 3 days ahead, freeze stock in 1-quart batches for ease of use.

TURKEY GRAVY

Preparation Time: 5 minutes
Start to Finish Time: 25 minutes
Serves: 2 (or 4)

Thanksgiving is incomplete without gravy. This recipe can be made ahead and refrigerated, easing the stress of day-of cooking. Reheat in a saucepan over low heat, or covered in the microwave.

2 (4) tablespoons butter
2 (4) tablespoons all-purpose flour
2 (4) cups turkey stock

(con't. next page)

Melt butter in a skillet over medium-high heat. Whisk in flour and keep whisking until fully incorporated and mixture has turned nearly dark brown. The color of this mixture, the roux, will help color the gravy. Slowly stir in the stock, whisking vigorously until smooth and the gravy has thickened. Taste and adjust with salt and pepper. Serve warm.

Variation:
Mushroom Gravy
Sauté ½ small onion (diced) and 4 ounces mushrooms (chopped) in 1 tablespoon butter until soft, about 10 minutes. Using just 1 tablespoon butter in the skillet, follow directions as above.

QUICK STOCK

Preparation Time: 5 minutes
Start to Finish Time: 40 minutes
Makes: About 1 cup

In a pinch and need a bit more stock? Doctoring up a canned broth is a good substitute. If not all ingredients are on hand, use what's available as anything can help improve the flavor. In a rush? Just 15 minutes of simmering can make a difference.

    1 (15-ounce) (or 2 cans) can chicken broth
    ½ (1) small onion, roughly chopped
    ½ (1) carrot, roughly chopped
    1 (2) parsley sprig

Put all ingredients in a small saucepan and bring to a boil over high heat. When boiling, reduce heat to low and simmer 30 minutes. Strain and discard solids. Use as needed.

CONNECT ON SOCIAL MEDIA

Let's connect!

Instagram: @cynthiagraubart

Facebook: @cynthiagraubartauthor

LinkedIn: @cynthiagraubart

See my online cooking classes
at cynthiagraubart.com

ABOUT THE AUTHOR

Cynthia Graubart is a James Beard Foundation Award-winning cookbook author and cooking teacher. Cynthia shares her passion for helping families spend more time at the dinner table together. She has appeared on Fox & Friends, Hallmark's Home & Family, NY1, syndicated Daytime TV Show, and frequently appears on morning shows.

Cynthia most recently authored her eighth cookbook, Sunday Suppers for Southern Living (2017) and will debut two new titles, Blueberry Love, and Strawberry love, in Spring 2021. She and Nathalie Dupree wrote the best-selling (and James Beard Foundation Award of Excellence-winning) Mastering the Art of Southern Cooking. Cynthia received a M.F.K. Fisher Food Writing Award for the introduction to Chicken: A Savor the South Cookbook.

Her work has appeared in the New York Times, Washington Post, Chicago Tribune, Los Angeles Times, Atlanta Journal Constitution, SeriousEats.com, Better Homes & Gardens, Southern Living, and Taste of the South, among many others.

Named a Georgia Grown Executive Chef for 2017 she joined her fellow appointees to cook at the James Beard House in June 2017. She co-led an all-female team of chefs in October 2019, also at the James Beard House, in celebration of Nathalie Dupree's 80th Birthday.

Cynthia is also a culinary television producer. With decades of experience behind her, Cynthia has produced live multi-camera television specials, in-studio culinary television series, and on-location packages. From producing, to directing, to editing, she has hands-on knowledge of every type of production environment, and she has produced more than a dozen pilot packages for renowned cookbook authors. She produced the ground-breaking nationally distributed cooking series Nathalie Dupree's New Southern Cooking and was nominated for a Georgia Emmy Award. She and colleague Chef Virginia Willis co-founded Culinary Media Training, a full-service training and production company aiding culinary professionals in telling their stories visually in all media.

Cynthia is a member of Les Dames d'Escoffier, a professional culinary organization with the mission to help foster the education of women in the culinary arts and related fields. She is a member of the Broadcast Committee for the James Beard Awards and is currently at work on two books in a new series cookbook series for Storey Publishers, a division of Workman.

Join Cynthia online at cynthiagraubart.com.

More Books by Cynthia Graubart

Sunday Suppers from Southern Living
Chicken: A Savor the South Cookbook
Mastering the Art of Southern Vegetables
Slow Cooker Double Dinners for Two
Slow Cooking For Two: Basics, Recipes, and Techniques
Mastering the Art of Southern Cooking
Southern Biscuits
The One-Armed Cook

Coming Spring 2020
Blueberry Love
Strawberry Love

Made in the USA
Columbia, SC
20 November 2020

25047277R00031